MONSTER MUSIC FESTIVALS
OZZFEST

GREG ROBISON

rosen publishing's
rosen central
New York

This one's for Kelly, Mom and Pop Robison, Bo, and Vu

Published in 2009 by The Rosen Publishing Group, Inc.
29 East 21st Street, New York, NY 10010

Copyright © 2009 by The Rosen Publishing Group, Inc.

First Edition

All rights reserved. No part of this book may be reproduced in any form without permission in writing from the publisher, except by a reviewer.

Library of Congress Cataloging-in-Publication Data

Robison, Greg.
Ozzfest / Greg Robison.—1st ed.
    p. cm.—(Monster music festivals)
Includes bibliographical references (p. 46) and index.
ISBN-13: 978-1-4042-1756-0 (library binding)
ISBN-13: 978-1-4358-5121-4 (pbk)
ISBN-13: 978-1-4042-7866-0 (6 pack)
1. Ozzfest—Juvenile literature. 2. Rock music festivals—Juvenile literature. I. Title.
ML36.O9 2009
781.66078—dc22

2007050751

Manufactured in Malaysia

On the cover: Foreground: Ozzy Osbourne (left) and Billy Idol. Background, top row, left to right: Chris Howorth of In This Moment in San Antonio, Texas, 2007; Ian Watkins of Lostprophets in Mountain View, California, 2002; Candace Kucsulain of Walls of Jericho in Mountain View, California, 2006; Rob Zombie in Mountain View, California, 2005. Background, left, top to bottom: Ozzy Osbourne in San Antonio, Texas, 2004; Marilyn Manson in Phoenix, Arizona, 2003.

CONTENTS

Introduction **4**

Chapter 1 **IN THE BEGINNING:**
THE HISTORY OF OZZFEST 7

Chapter 2 **BRINGING METAL TO THE MASSES:**
THE OZZFEST SETTING 16

Chapter 3 **LOVE IT LOUD:**
THE PEOPLE AT OZZFEST 25

Chapter 4 **I WANT TO ROCK:**
THE OZZFEST EXPERIENCE 32

Chapter 5 **COUNT ME IN: HOW YOU CAN ATTEND**
AN OZZFEST SHOW 39

Glossary **43**
For More Information **44**
For Further Reading **45**
Bibliography **46**
Index **47**

INTRODUCTION

Ozzy Osbourne *(left)* performs at Ozzfest 2000. Slayer *(above)* rocks the arena at Ozzfest 2004. Check out that wall of Marshall amplifiers!

Do you like your music a bit heavier? When you listen to your iPod, is your motto, "If it's too loud, you're too old"? Is the mosh pit your favorite place at a concert? If you answered yes to any of these questions, then the annual Ozzfest may be just the music festival for you.

Morgan Lander, lead singer of the all-female metal band Kittie, sums up the uniqueness of Ozzfest when she says, "This festival provides bands like ours the opportunity to bring metal to the mainstream masses." She's right. In 2007, Ozzfest celebrated its eleventh year on the road. It's the second-longest-running touring festival in North America. (The Vans Warped Tour has been on the road one year longer.) In addition, Ozzfest has brought a smile to many international headbangers, playing shows in central Europe and the United Kingdom, including the prestigious Download Festival in England.

The annual Ozzfest tour is organized by the "Godfather of Metal," Ozzy Osbourne, and his wife, Sharon Osbourne. Through the years, the tour has featured performances by legendary heavy metal bands such as Black Sabbath, Iron Maiden, Pantera, Judas Priest, Slayer, Fear Factory, Motörhead, and Tool. Metal maniacs around the globe have been

OZZFEST

introduced to artists such as Kittie, Disturbed, Slipknot, Static-X, Incubus, and Type O Negative, all of which have appeared on the famous Ozzfest "second stage." And what would the festival be without an appearance by the man who puts the "Ozz" in Ozzfest? Ozzy himself generally closes the show with his amazing live set.

In addition to the great music, Ozzfest gives you the opportunity to shop for your favorite heavy metal merchandise from vendors located throughout the festival. Or, you can check out the fantastic tattoos and other body art on display from some of the best artists in the world. For these and many other reasons, Ozzfest has become one of the most anticipated shows of the year for heavy metal fans all over the world. Pack your earplugs and read on to find out more about this monster of a music festival.

Chapter 1

In the Beginning:
The History of Ozzfest

Heavy metal fans across the world should send the organizers of the Lollapalooza music festival a thank-you card. In 1996, they refused to let Ozzy Osbourne join their tour, saying that Ozzy was "uncool" and past his prime. But Ozzy didn't pack up and go home. Instead, he and wife, Sharon, decided to create their own music festival—one where they would have the final say in which bands would play. They didn't know who would be on the bill, but you can be sure they knew it was going to be very loud, very heavy, and very cool.

Let There Be Rock: The First Ozzfest Festival

The very first Ozzfest festival cranked it up on October 26, 1996, at the Blockbuster Desert Sky Pavilion in Phoenix, Arizona.

7

OZZFEST

Powerman 5000 generated buzz while playing on the second stage at the very first Ozzfest in 1996. The following year, the band moved up to play the main stage.

That concert was followed by a second show on October 27, at the Glen Helen Blockbuster Pavilion in Devore, California. The all-day festival was basically a "who's who" of the hottest heavy metal acts at the time. Bands playing the main stage included Danzig, Slayer, Prong, Sepultura, Fear Factory, Biohazard, and Ozzy.

IN THE BEGINNING: THE HISTORY OF OZZFEST

The concerts also featured a "second stage," where up-and-coming metal bands could rock the house. Rocking sets by such bands as Coal Chamber, Powerman 5000, Neurosis, and Earth Crisis made the second stage an immediate hit, and it has been featured on all Ozzfest shows since. To the surprise of no one, Ozzfest was a huge success, playing to capacity crowds at both shows. Finally, the heavy metal community had a festival that it could proudly call its own.

If It's Too Loud, You're Too Old: The Music of Ozzfest

One thing you are certain not to hear at an Ozzfest show is, "Can you turn it down, please?" The bands featured on this tour, along with their fans, love music played loud. In case you don't know, the heavy metal way of doing things is to turn the volume all the way up. Or beyond. David St. Hubbins, the guitarist of the fictional band in the movie *This Is Spinal Tap*, neatly sums up the metal attitude in four little words. When showing his interviewer how loud his band's amps are, he proudly points out, "These go to 11!"

Just what is heavy metal? Typically, it is thought of as the most aggressive and extreme form of rock music. But, as Rob Halford, lead singer of Judas Priest, notes, heavy metal "is not just about the music—it's a way of life." Within the category, or genre, of heavy metal, there are many styles. Here are some of

OZZFEST

the different subgenres of metal that you can expect to come across at Ozzfest:

- **Traditional metal:** "Old school" heavy metal played by music legends (examples: Black Sabbath, Ozzy Osbourne, Judas Priest).
- **NWOBHM:** This is an abbreviation for "new wave of British heavy metal." It was made popular by loud, fast, and aggressive bands hailing from the United Kingdom in the 1980s (examples: Iron Maiden, Motörhead).
- **Speed metal:** Also called thrash metal, this type of metal features incredibly fast guitar riffs and double-bass drumming (examples: Slayer, Megadeth).
- **Black metal:** This subgenre features dark lyrics, both screaming and "clean" vocals, and heavy, haunting music (examples: Cradle of Filth, Dimmu Borgir).
- **Nu metal:** Heavy, down-tuned guitars combined with loud vocals and rap-core make up the sounds of nu metal (examples: Korn, Linkin Park, Drowning Pool).

Some bands and performers, like Fear Factory, Kittie, Pantera, Tool, and Rob Zombie, can be classified under several

IN THE BEGINNING: THE HISTORY OF OZZFEST

Here are the members of the mighty Black Sabbath, photographed in 1970: *(from left)* Bill Ward, Tony Iommi, Ozzy Osbourne, and Geezer Butler.

of these subgenres. As you can see, there is definitely something for every heavy metal fan at Ozzfest.

Meet Ozzy Osbourne: The Godfather of Heavy Metal

Ozzy Osbourne really doesn't need an introduction. He is the cofounder of Ozzfest, lead singer of his own band, and still very

OZZFEST

involved with heavy metal pioneers Black Sabbath. Somehow, he has also found the time to star in the hit MTV reality series *The Osbournes*.

In 1948, John Michael Osbourne was born in Birmingham, England. Ever since he was very young, music was always a major factor in his life. In 1968, Ozzy formed the band Earth, with former schoolmates Terry "Geezer" Butler, Tony Iommi, and Bill Ward. The band evolved into Black Sabbath, which is regularly cited as the most important and influential heavy metal band of all time. After recording numerous gold and platinum records with the band, Ozzy left Black Sabbath in 1979 to pursue a solo career.

When Ozzy decided to set off on his own, he needed to find a new manager to help him with his business affairs. Sharon Arden, daughter of Black Sabbath manager Don Arden, was about to start her own management company and decided to take on Ozzy as a client. In Ozzy, Sharon saw a solo artist with tremendous potential, based on his outgoing personality and the electric live shows he pulled off during his time with Black Sabbath. She was right. Ozzy's first solo album was a hit, and his albums and tours since then have continued to be huge successes worldwide.

In 1997, Ozzy and his old mates in Black Sabbath decided to get together for several Ozzfest shows. Inspired by the tremendous response they received, the band decided to reunite and tour the world. To the delight of metal fans everywhere,

IN THE BEGINNING: THE HISTORY OF OZZFEST

Black Sabbath also went on to record a new live album—their first with Ozzy in more than a decade—and appear on several more Ozzfest tours.

Television helped introduce Ozzy to people not familiar with his music. MTV, the music television network, sent a camera crew to his family's mansion in Los Angeles, California, to film the singer, Sharon, and two of their children, Kelly and Jack. *The Osbournes* debuted in 2002 and turned out to be one of the biggest successes in MTV history, with millions of fans tuning in regularly to watch the adventures of this first family of heavy metal.

Ozzy's legendary live shows, along with outrageous antics both on and off stage, have earned him the nickname the "Prince of Darkness." In the real world, however, he is a family man,

The Osbournes, an MTV reality show featuring Ozzy and his family, brought the singer a new level of fame—and notoriety.

OZZFEST

With her fun-loving attitude and sharp opinions, Sharon Osbourne has become a popular television personality in the United Kingdom and the United States.

and he has always tried to remain modest.

Meet Sharon Osbourne: Living Life to the Extreme

Sharon Osbourne is the wife and personal manager of Ozzy Osbourne, as well as the proud mom of three children and one stepson. She is also the cofounder of Ozzfest, runs a record label (Divine Recordings), and has served as manager for several bands. You may have also seen her on the MTV hit reality show *The Osbournes* or in one of her many television appearances.

Sharon Arden was born in 1952 in London, England. She grew up around the entertainment industry: Her father, Don, was a music manager and founder of the Jet Records label, and her mother, Hope, was a professional dancer. Sharon decided to

IN THE BEGINNING: THE HISTORY OF OZZFEST

enter the music business at an early age. In fact, she was still in her teens when she began working for her father's management company. A major turning point in her life occurred soon after, when she became the personal manager of Ozzy Osbourne.

With a combination of hard work, determination, and sheer will, Sharon helped Ozzy become one of the world's most popular metal acts. At the same time, she started to make a name for herself in the industry. In 1996, she and Ozzy founded Ozzfest, the wildly popular annual touring festival. Under her watchful guidance, Ozzfest has become one of the biggest and most successful touring music festivals in the world today. Many bands have been propelled to superstardom following appearances at Ozzfest, including Marilyn Manson, Black Label Society, and Slipknot. In addition to managing Ozzy, Sharon has also managed bands such as Coal Chamber, ELO, Gary Moore, Motörhead, and Smashing Pumpkins. The popular rock magazine *Kerrang!* voted Sharon Osbourne "the most important person in rock" in 2004.

Sharon Osbourne has enjoyed huge success in the music and entertainment industry. But family comes first. She's the proud mother of three children: Aimee, Jack, and Kelly. Additionally, she has a stepson, Robert Marcato, whom she and Ozzy adopted after Robert's mother—a close friend of Sharon's—passed away.

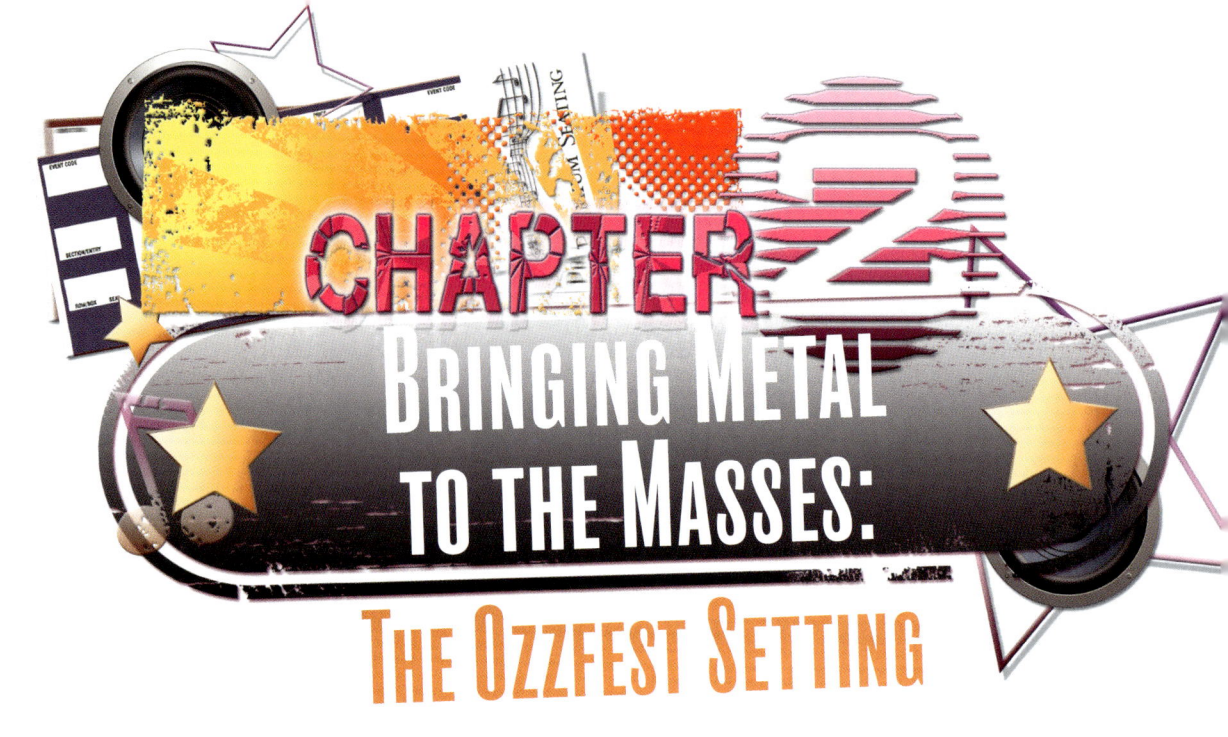

Chapter 2
Bringing Metal to the Masses:
The Ozzfest Setting

As summer approaches, metal fans everywhere prepare for the arrival of Ozzfest. Since its first year in 1996 when the festival played just two shows, Ozzfest has grown to an annual touring festival, making appearances all across North America and Europe.

Where's Ozzy?: Where the Ozzfest Takes Place

The Ozzfest festival is a "tour in a box." This means the sound systems, lights, musical equipment, stages, merchandise, and vendor and concession booths—and, of course, the bands—all travel with the tour. Generally, the venue is a music hall, coliseum, or athletic stadium. For example, if you lived in San Antonio, Texas, you would have checked out the 2007 tour

BRINGING METAL TO THE MASSES: THE OZZFEST SETTING

Heavy rockers Chevelle tear into it at Ozzfest 2005. The stages at Ozzfest feature high-end lighting and sound production, so your favorite bands will look and sound great.

at the Verizon Wireless Amphitheatre. If you lived in Detroit, Michigan, the DTE Energy Music Theatre was the place to be.

If you are a musician in an Ozzfest band or someone working on the Ozzfest tour, you will really know what it is like to be "on the road." Ozzfest generally begins in the middle of July and runs through late August. The North American leg

OZZFEST

of the tour usually starts on the West Coast and concludes on the East Coast. In Europe, the tour has traveled to Germany, the United Kingdom, the Netherlands, Belgium, Portugal, Poland, and the Czech Republic. The number of show dates on Ozzfest varies from year to year. In 2007, twenty-four dates were played in forty-nine days, to almost 500,000 people in North America.

Come Early and Stay Late: What You Can See and Do at Ozzfest

If you and your friends decide to go to Ozzfest, be sure to get plenty of rest the night before the show. You have a very busy day ahead of you.

Before you head out to the festival, here are a few suggestions for a safe and enjoyable time. Be sure to bring enough cash for drinks, food, and a souvenir or two. Most vendors on the tour accept major credit and debit cards, too. If the show is being held outdoors, check the weather report before you go. If it's going to be hot, don't forget the sunscreen and a hat. If it looks like rain, stash a poncho and an extra T-shirt and shorts in your backpack. Wear comfy shoes and pack lightly because you will be doing a lot of walking around. Pack a pair of earplugs just in case the show gets too loud. You might think earplugs aren't very cool, but wearing them is much cooler than damaging your hearing. Don't forget to charge your cell phone and bring

BRINGING METAL TO THE MASSES: THE OZZFEST SETTING

it with you. If you don't have a phone, bring change for a pay phone. Make sure that you have a ride home from the festival if you're not driving, and be sure your ride knows exactly when and where to pick you up. Finally, don't forget your tickets. If you are picking up your tickets at the venue, call beforehand to find out where the will-call window is located.

Meeting your favorite band is always a big thrill. Here, Wayne Static of Static-X signs some autographs for lucky Ozzfest fans in Devore, California.

Once inside the gates at Ozzfest, you can shop for your favorite band's T-shirt, CD, or other items from the many vendor booths that are on the tour. In addition, many organizations have booths where you can learn about different causes and charities. Get out of the pit and recharge with an energy drink or water, and cool off in one of the misting tents. If you're hungry, grab something to eat between bands from one of the many food vendors.

OZZFEST

If your timing is right, you can attend one of the "meet and greets" organized by the vendors, record labels, and tour sponsors of Ozzfest. For these events, band members come to the sponsor's booth, sign autographs, and say hello to their fans.

And, of course, there is the music.

Metal for All

One of the reasons that Ozzfest is so popular with heavy metal fans is that there are so many different bands to see at the show. Whatever your preferred type of metal, chances are that one of your favorite bands has performed at Ozzfest.

With bands from all over the world hoping for a spot on the tour, the selection process is anything but easy. Just about all of the booking agents, record labels, and management teams associated with heavy metal want their band on the tour. The reason is that each band will play to thousands of people each day and will receive a great deal of exposure. The buzz generated by playing Ozzfest is so valuable, many record labels and management companies offer to pay Ozzfest in order to have their band appear on the tour. Although there are many people associated with Ozzfest, Sharon and Ozzy Osbourne make the ultimate decision as to which bands are selected.

The annual lineup for Ozzfest is usually announced several months before the tour begins. Fans can check with the official Ozzfest Web site (http://www.ozzfest.com) for regular updates.

BRINGING METAL TO THE MASSES: THE OZZFEST SETTING

You can also scope out your favorite band's Web site to see if they are appearing on the tour. Here's a list of just a handful of the bands that have played Ozzfest:

- Rob Zombie
- Slipknot
- Pantera
- Slayer
- System of a Down
- Korn
- Black Label Society
- Kittie
- Tool
- Godsmack
- Iron Maiden

"Dimebag" Darrell Abbott of Pantera shreds at Ozzfest 1997. Bands love the rush of playing in front of the tour's enthusiastic crowds.

OZZFEST

Battle for Ozzfest

In 2004, Ozzy and Sharon Osbourne came up with a novel idea for selecting an unknown band to appear on the Ozzfest tour. They invited bands from all over the world to audition for one of eight contestant slots on a reality show called *Battle for Ozzfest*. Once the finalists were selected, individual members from each of the bands were filmed performing various challenges that tested their rock-and-roll mettle. Then, after the show, viewers and fans voted online to eliminate one contestant. During the twelfth and final episode, nearly two million fans cast their votes online for one of the two remaining contestants. In the end, Marc, the guitarist from Texas band A Dozen Furies, was the last contestant standing. His lucky band received $60,000, a ton of new musical gear, a chance at a record deal with Sanctuary Records, and, most important, a spot on the 2005 Ozzfest tour!

Fifteen to twenty-five bands usually perform each day at Ozzfest, so a ton of planning and hard work is needed to get the festival ready to go. Setup begins very early in the morning, with tour personnel rushing to build stages, load in production gear and musical equipment, and assemble sound and lighting rigs. At the same time, vendors are busy setting up their booths.

BRINGING METAL TO THE MASSES: THE OZZFEST SETTING

Bands on the second stage usually perform between twenty and thirty-five minutes, while bands on the main stage generally play sets ranging from forty-five to ninety minutes, depending on the time slot. Performance times are usually from 9:00 AM to 11:00 PM each day.

The Ozzfest main stage and second stage are the major focal points of the festival. The second stage usually turns over faster because the bands on the main stage generally have more gear and play longer sets. It takes a lot of coordination and planning to make sure everyone's set goes smoothly. The bands and their road crews have to work fast to get their gear and instruments on the stage before their performance and off the stage quickly when they are finished so that they don't slow down the next band.

"Freefest": Ozzfest 2007 Gives Back to the Fans

It's every heavy metal fan's dream—an opportunity to see Ozzfest free of charge. Sometimes, festivals will hold contests giving lucky fans a chance to win free tickets to a show, and bands occasionally perform a free concert. But who's ever heard of an entire free tour? In February 2007, Ozzy and Sharon Osbourne announced that the tickets for the 2007 Ozzfest would be free. Fans couldn't just show up at the show and expect to get in, though. Tickets were available through sponsor Web sites, the official Ozzfest Web site, and to those

OZZFEST

"Freefest!" At the Concert Industry Consortium in Los Angeles, California, Ozzy and Sharon Osbourne announce the exciting news that Ozzfest 2007 will be free.

who purchased an advance copy of Ozzy's new *Black Rain* CD. Many industry insiders said that a free tour simply wouldn't work, but the Osbournes and the fans of Ozzfest proved them wrong. Over four days, LiveNation.com distributed more than 428,000 tickets for the tour's twenty-four shows to lucky fans around the country. It was the largest number of free concert tickets ever distributed in the United States.

CHAPTER 3

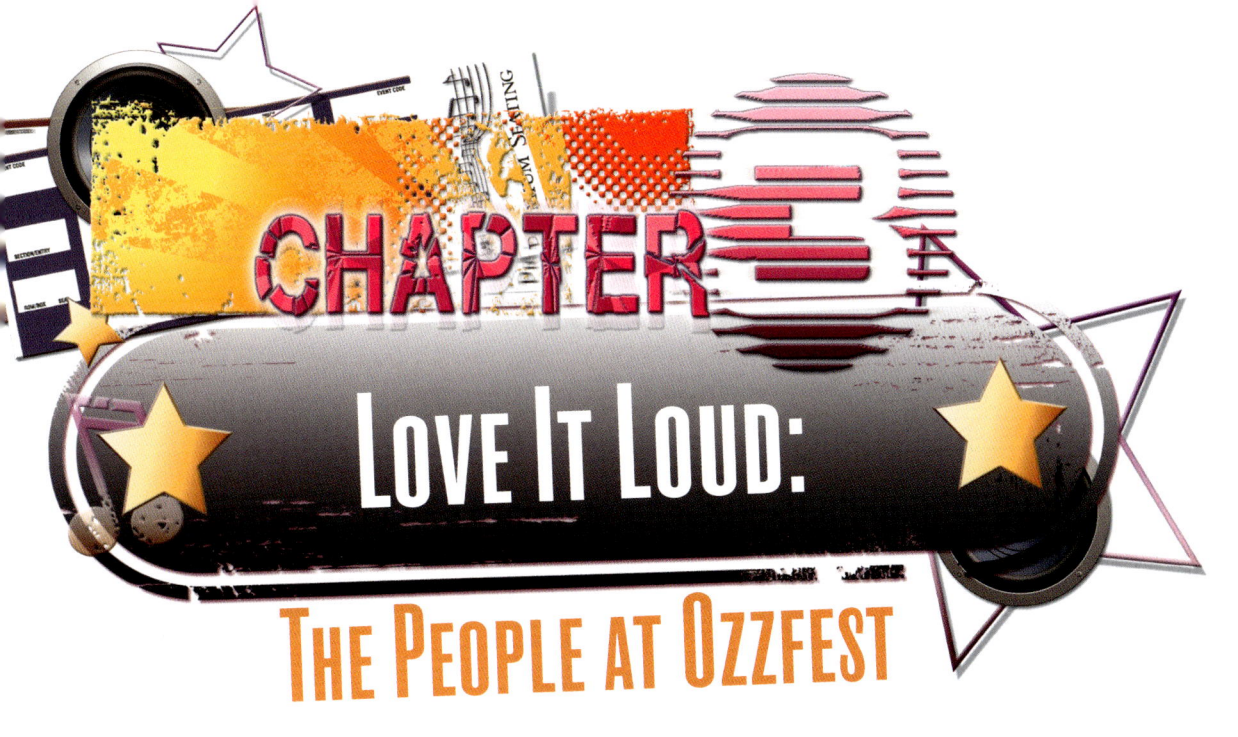

Love It Loud: The People at Ozzfest

If you like being part of a big crowd, then Ozzfest is the tour for you. Almost 500,000 fans in North America experienced the tour in 2007, not including the bands and support personnel that travel with the tour, or employees of the local venue.

Making It Happen: The People and Jobs on Ozzfest

Ozzy Osbourne's job is to rock the crowd every night. Sharon Osbourne's job is to organize the festival and make sure everything runs smoothly. But in addition to Ozzy and Sharon, several hundred people work hard to make Ozzfest successful. Who are some of these people, and what do they do?

- **Tour promoters:** Promoters are the people who bring Ozzfest to your town. They work with the

OZZFEST

A lot of hard work goes on behind the scenes at Ozzfest so that you can have a great time. Here, fans rock out in Mountain View, California, in 2007.

tour to set up the time and date of the show, and they decide on where the show is going to be held. In addition, they work with local radio stations, television stations, and sponsors to ensure that the show is being advertised. They send out tour posters and postcards to music-related businesses. Sometimes, they sponsor contests where you can win tickets to a show on the tour or VIP passes. Their job is to make sure there are lots of people at the show.

- **Tour truck drivers:** It takes great drivers to get the tour from one place to another. A fleet of tour buses, semitrucks, and tractor-trailer trucks are needed to transport the bands, tour personnel, and equipment

LOVE IT LOUD: THE PEOPLE AT OZZFEST

from one tour stop to the next. Professional drivers have to go to school to learn how to drive these huge vehicles and earn their commercial driver's license. Additionally, they must have safe driving records. Tour drivers regularly drive between 200 and 500 miles (approximately 320 to 800 kilometers) each night. They generally sleep during the day and drive all night so that they arrive at the next tour stop bright and early each morning.

Tattoo Artists

You will find some of the best tattoo artists from all over the world traveling with the Ozzfest tour. Check out their booths to see some truly amazing body art.

These are not temporary tattoos! If you are considering getting a tattoo one day, be sure that you love the design and can live with it for a long time. Also, if you are under the age of eighteen, you must have a parent's written permission before you can get a tattoo.

Jason Miller of the band Godhead shows off his ink.

OZZFEST

- **Sound engineers:** These folks are responsible for making sure the bands sound great on stage. It's not easy getting great sound when the volume levels are so high, but Ozzfest sound engineers work with state-of-the-art production equipment and always get the bands to sound their best.
- **Tour security:** This is a very important job at Ozzfest. Security personnel ensure the safety of the bands, the fans, and the tour equipment.

These burly security workers have their hands full containing the mosh pit at Ozzfest 2007 in San Antonio, Texas.

LOVE IT LOUD: THE PEOPLE AT OZZFEST

- **Merchandise vendors:** Merchandise vendors set up their booths to display their products, and they handle the cash and credit cards when a purchase is made. When a band comes to a vendor booth to do a "meet and greet," it can get extremely busy.
- **Tour caterers:** Tour caterers make sure that no one at Ozzfest goes hungry. They travel with their own portable kitchen and prepare meals for hundreds of people each day. Breakfast, lunch, dinner, and snacks are provided for the bands and crew every day, so the catering staff is always busy.
- **First-aid tent personnel:** Always open during the show, the people working in the first-aid tent can help you out in many ways. They'll treat your minor injuries, make sure that you are hydrated with plenty of water or an energy drink, or just give you a place to lie down and cool off. If you get banged up in the mosh pit or if you are feeling overheated, visit the first-aid tent. They will have you up and banging your head again in no time.

United We Stand: Who Attends Ozzfest?

When asked why he loves playing Ozzfest, Jonathan Davis, lead singer of Korn, singles out the "amazing" fans. There are a lot of fans attending Ozzfest each year. In fact, between

OZZFEST

400,000 and 500,000 North American fans have attended Ozzfest in each of the last few years. Also, the tour has traveled to the United Kingdom four times, playing to large, enthusiastic crowds there. About 15,000 to 17,000 people attend each Ozzfest show, and there are generally twenty to twenty-five shows on the American tour each year.

Who's coming out to the shows? People aged seventeen to twenty-four make up the majority of the audience, with an almost even split between males and females. However, as Ozzfest is an all-ages show, you will see many different types of fans on the tour. So, don't be surprised if you see a thirteen-year-old fan in a Marilyn Manson T-shirt in the audience next to a forty-year-old father of two who's there to support Black Sabbath.

Ozzfest is all about the fans for Jonathan Davis, lead singer of Korn. He is shown here rocking the Phoenix, Arizona, crowd on the Ozzfest 2003 tour.

LOVE IT LOUD: THE PEOPLE AT OZZFEST

Ozzfest attendees are big music fans who come out to support their favorite metal bands. But many Ozzfest attendees are also there to check out the latest in hard rock fashion apparel and to soak up the heavy metal culture of the festival.

Ozzfest and the Media

If you don't think that you will be able to catch Ozzfest live, you can keep up with the latest tour updates on television. Tune in to cable channels Fuse, MTV, CNN, Musique Plus, and Much Music (Canada's Music Channel) for updates and coverage. Check your local news networks as well. In addition, you can read about Ozzfest in *Revolver*, *Metal Maniacs*, *Metal Hammer*, *Rolling Stone*, *Spin*, *Newsweek*, *Time*, and *Billboard* magazines. Or, turn on your computer to keep up with your favorite band on the tour. Check out Live Nation, MySpace, MTV Online, Fanscape, Billboard Online, Pollstar, and the official Ozzfest Web site, www.ozzfest.com.

Chapter 4
I Want to Rock:
The Ozzfest Experience

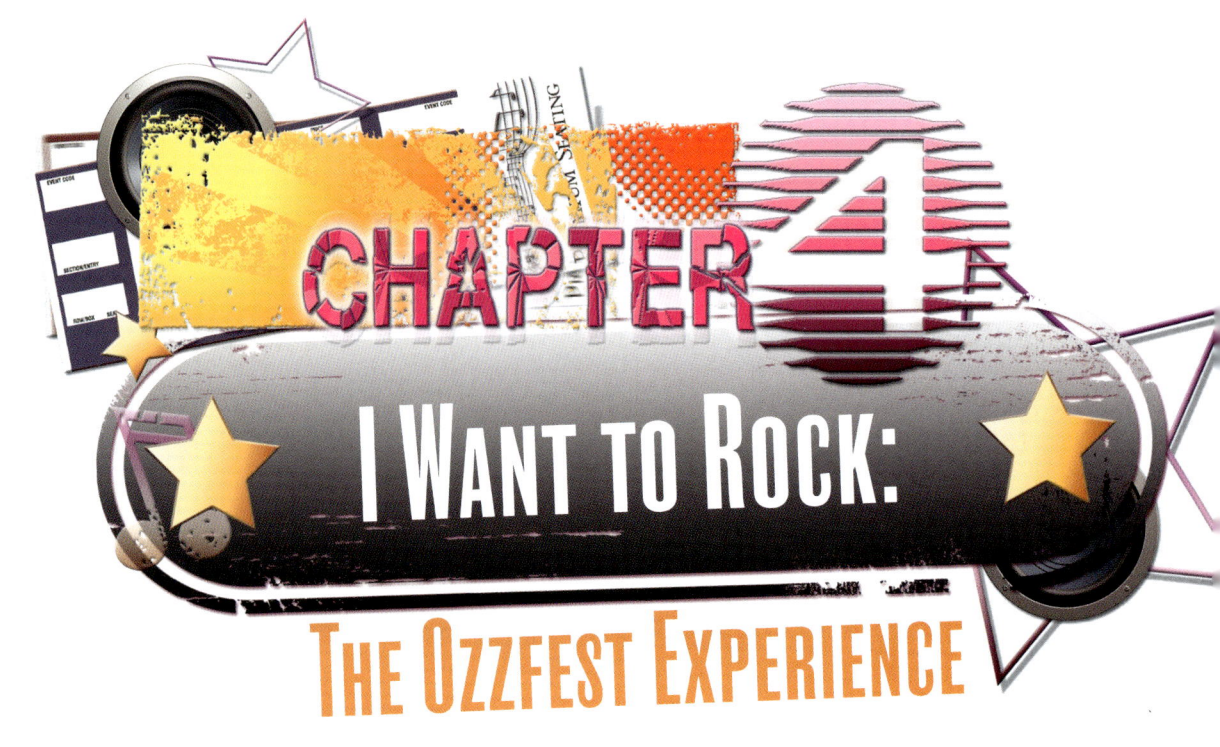

For many people, heavy metal is not just another type of music—it's a way of life. To these folks, Ozzfest is an annual tradition. Many parents bring their kids out to the show. Older brothers and sisters let younger siblings come to the tour with them and show them how to rock. Fans plan summer vacations around tour dates they want to attend. And some serious headbangers even follow the tour from city to city, or around the world.

It's a big honor to be chosen as one of the bands that will play Ozzfest. Many young musicians have been inspired by the legendary bands they have had the opportunity to play with at Ozzfest, including Black Sabbath, Iron Maiden, Judas Priest, and Pantera. It's a lot of hard work on the tour, but it's an opportunity to have a lot of fun as well. Read on to learn more about the experiences that these people had.

I WANT TO ROCK: THE OZZFEST EXPERIENCE

The Band Experience

To find out what it's like to be one of the bands invited to tour with Ozzfest, we talked with sisters Morgan and Mercedes Lander, the founding members of Kittie. The band was a part of the 2000 North American tour, as well as the 2002 European tour. In this exclusive interview, they talk about some of their experiences on Ozzfest.

Morgan Lander *(left)* and Mercedes Lander are the founding members of Kittie. They started the band while they were still in high school.

Greg Robison: How did you become involved with Ozzfest?

Morgan Lander: I remember we were sitting at the dinner table with our parents back home in Canada, and the phone rang. It was a representative from Ozzfest, asking if we were interested in playing on the tour, and could we send them a press kit for them to review. Needless to say, we were pretty excited but didn't know what to expect.

Mercedes Lander: We were touring in England when we got the call that we were going to officially be on the tour. We were all jumping up and down and screaming! It was exciting.

GR: What was your favorite experience on Ozzfest?

Morgan: Being able to watch Pantera every night was awesome. And, in 2000, it was a thrill to be featured on the cover of *Kerrang!* magazine's annual Ozzfest issue.

Mercedes: The sense of unity between bands was amazing. It was really cool how the veteran bands would hang out with the younger bands, and inspiring as well. Also, the crowds were incredible. We played in front of so many people!

GR: Do you have any advice to bands that aspire to play on Ozzfest?

Morgan: Expect to have a great time! Have a sense of humor and be ready for anything. The great part of the music business is that grown men and women can still act like kids. It was almost like high school again when we were out on Ozzfest.

I WANT TO ROCK: THE OZZFEST EXPERIENCE

Mercedes: Practice, practice, practice! Make a name for yourself and gain the support of a record label or management company. You will have a great time on Ozzfest. It's like one big family out on the road.

The Fan Experience

Brent Z. has been in the music industry for almost twenty years. He is also a big fan of heavy metal music. In this interview, Brent recounts some of his memories of Ozzfest.

Greg Robison: When and where did you attend Ozzfest?

Brent Z.: I have attended a few Ozzfest shows. In 1997, I saw the Texas Ozzfest dates, and in 1999, I saw Ozzfest in Atlanta, Georgia.

GR: Describe the setting of Ozzfest. What really stood out for you?

BZ: Both years I went the shows were very well attended. There were just people everywhere, kind of an organized chaos, almost like a heavy metal picnic or a misfit family outing.

GR: Besides the bands, did you have a favorite exhibit or vendor booth?

OZZFEST

The "Ozz Man" wows the crowd during an Ozzfest appearance in 1997. When both Ozzy and Black Sabbath perform at Ozzfest, Ozzy performs two full sets.

BZ: The music was where the real value was for me. I do recall the rock-climbing wall, though . . . It was good fun seeing all the young metal kids decked out in their gear (leather gauntlets, bandannas, studded belts) trying to scale that thing.

GR: What was your overall opinion of Ozzfest?

BZ: My main thought at the time was—metal is back! After being overshadowed by radio metal, "hair metal" (with all its lame ballads), alternative rock, the grunge rock movement, etc., in the late 1980s and early 1990s, I thought, "This is more like it!" It was about time for the return of some good metal into the culture of music.

I WANT TO ROCK: THE OZZFEST EXPERIENCE

The Very First Ozzfest: A Band Experience

Tommy Victor needs no introduction in the heavy metal world. As lead singer and guitarist for the band Prong, he's had his share of huge shows and festivals. In 1996, he was touring with the band Danzig, who was on the main stage for the very first Ozzfest shows. Victor shares some memories of those shows in this exclusive interview.

Greg Robison: How did you become involved with Ozzfest?

Tommy Victor: My band Prong opened for Ozzy in 1995, the year before Ozzfest began. When the first Ozzfest came along in 1996, I was playing guitar in the band Danzig and played the festival with them.

GR: What was your favorite experience playing Ozzfest?

TV: It was great playing with Ozzy. Also, Sharon Osbourne has always been good to me and to Prong. She was very involved at our old record label (Epic Records), as Ozzy was on that label also. Our relationship goes way back before Ozzfest.

GR: What was your biggest challenge at Ozzfest?

OZZFEST

TV: The weather! We had a huge problem with the wind and dust at one of our shows. On the main stage, we were literally getting whipped with gusts of wind and sand!

GR: What was your favorite band that you played with on Ozzfest?

TV: I enjoyed getting to see newcomers such as Powerman 5000 and old favorites like Neurosis sharing a stage.

Tommy Victor, lead singer and guitarist of Prong, is an Ozzfest veteran. He has also worked with Danzig, Rob Zombie, Marilyn Manson, and Ministry.

GR: Do you have any advice to a band that is aspiring to play Ozzfest?

TV: Well, Ozzfest has changed a lot since those first shows. These days, Ozzfest seems to work well for bands that are getting airplay on the radio. It also helps if you have a look that sets you apart from other bands in the crowd.

CHAPTER 5

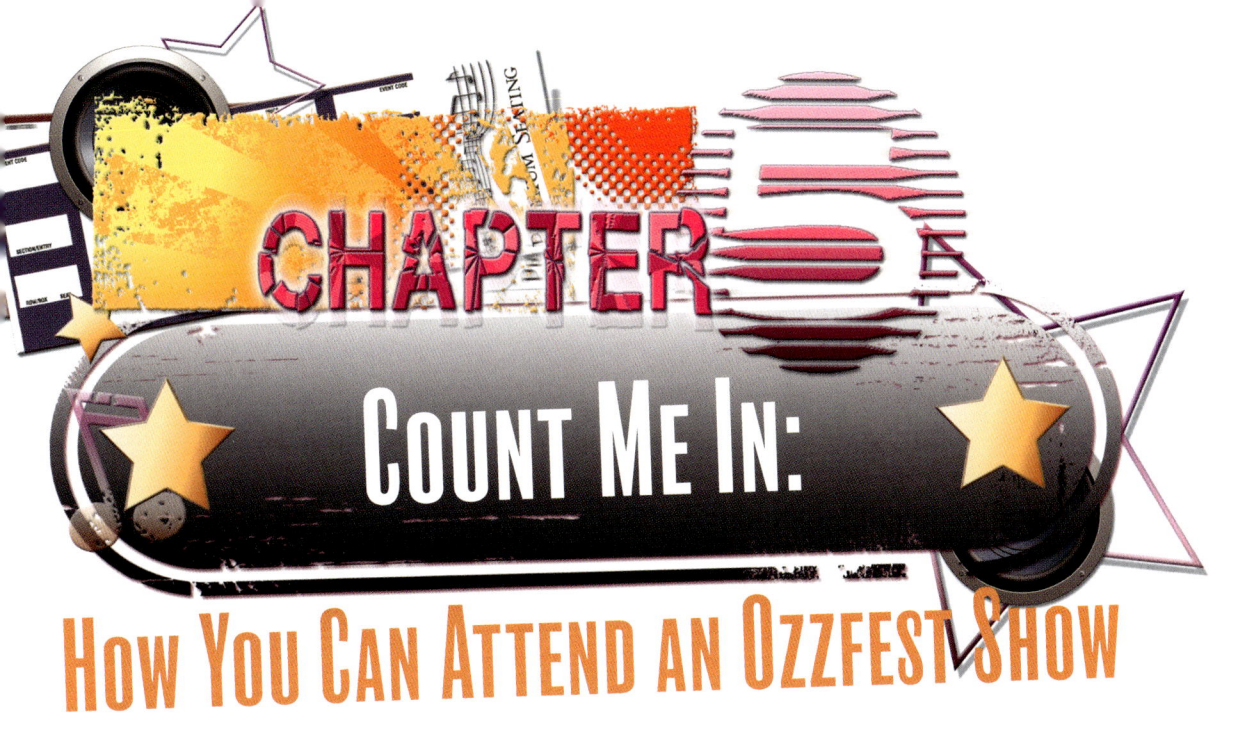

Count Me In:

How You Can Attend an Ozzfest Show

More than a dozen years after it first hit the road, Ozzfest shows no signs of slowing down. Maybe after reading this book, you'll decide to check out Ozzfest for yourself. In that case, the official Ozzfest Web site (http://www.ozzfest.com) is the best place to go. The site is updated all year long, so it will keep you in the know as to who is slated to play on the tour, and it will keep you up to date on special contests and events. It's also a great place to check out the latest news in the world of heavy metal. Most important, the Web site is where you can preorder tickets to the show of your choice before they even go on sale to the general public.

Once the tour route and lineup are set (generally in late spring), this information is posted on the Web site, along with instructions on how to preorder tickets. If you are planning to preorder, you will need to pay by credit card. Also, check back

OZZFEST

Here is the home page of the official Ozzfest Web site (www.ozzfest.com). In addition to posting the latest Ozzfest news, the site has links to the Ozzfest store and a fan chat forum.

often, as there are contests throughout the year that give you a shot at winning tickets, VIP passes, and other great swag.

If you are not able to preorder, you may still be able to get tickets up to the day of the show at Ticketmaster outlets. Ticketmaster is one of the largest ticket sales companies in the world, providing tickets to concerts, sporting events, and plays. Check http://www.ticketmaster.com or your local Yellow Pages

COUNT ME IN: HOW YOU CAN ATTEND AN OZZFEST SHOW

to see where its closest location is to you. Another ticket source is the venue box office where the Ozzfest will be held. Give them a call and they can tell you about ticket availability.

If you decide at the last minute that you want to go to Ozzfest, you may be able to purchase tickets the day of the show at the venue box office. Ozzfest usually does sell out, but the venue may release a limited number of tickets the day of the show.

If you don't have tickets for the show, listen to your local hard rock radio station—they often have ticket giveaways to help promote the show. You can also go to http://www.ozzfest.com and check for ticket giveaway contests. You never know—Ozzy and Sharon may decide to make a future Ozzfest tour a "Freefest," as they did in 2007.

While You Are Waiting on Ozzfest: Other Festivals to Check Out

The bad news is that Ozzfest comes around only once a year. But there is good news as well. If you like Ozzfest, then there are several other festivals that you may want to check out:

Rockstar Taste of Chaos

If you like your music loud and heavy, the Rockstar Taste of Chaos Tour may be for you. This tour is the brainchild of music industry veterans Kevin Lyman, John Reese, and Darryl

OZZFEST

Hard rock fans in Sydney, Australia, enjoy the sights and sounds of the Rockstar Taste of Chaos Tour in 2006. G'day mate!

Eaton. The 2007 Taste of Chaos Tour exceeded all expectations, selling 360,000 tickets in North America and 86,000 internationally. Visit the official Taste of Chaos Web site (http://www.tasteofchaos.com) for details and updates.

Family Values Tour

The Family Values Tour offers you a chance to check out different genres of heavy metal, including nu metal, alternative metal, hard rock, and even rap music. Founded by the band Korn, the tour rocked through North America in 1998, 1999, and 2001. After a four-year absence, hard rockers around the country welcomed the tour back with open arms. Check with the Family Values official Web site (http://www.familyvalueslive.com) for updates.

GLOSSARY

aggressive Assertive, bold, and energetic.
apparel Clothing.
capacity The maximum amount that can be contained.
coordination Harmonious combination or interaction.
exceed To be greater than; to surpass.
exclusive Not divided or shared with others.
genre Type or category.
inclusive Including much or everything.
influential One that is of considerable importance or influence.
laurels Honors, or recognition for something good.
legendary Extremely well known, famous, or renowned.
mainstream The principal or dominant course, tendency, or trend.
mettle Vigor and strength of spirit.
mosh pit Area at a concert, usually directly in front of the stage, where people dance by pushing and slamming into each other.
personnel A body of persons employed in an organization or place of work.
prestigious Honored.
souvenir A token of remembrance, a memento.
subgenre More narrowly defined category within a type or genre.
venue Locale or place.

For More Information

Kerrang! Magazine
Mappin House
4 Winsley Street
London W1W 8HF
England
Web site: http://www.kerrang.com
Kerrang! is the top-selling weekly rock magazine. The magazine sponsors a stage at Ozzfest and publishes an annual Ozzfest edition.

Ticketmaster
1000 Corporate Landing
Charleston, WV 25311
Web site: http://www.ticketmaster.com
Ticketmaster has been providing ticket services, marketing, and distribution of event tickets and information for more than thirty years.

Web Sites

Due to the changing nature of Internet links, Rosen Publishing has developed an online list of Web sites related to the subject of this book. This site is updated regularly. Please use this link to access the list:

http://www.rosenlinks.com/mmf/ozzf

FOR FURTHER READING

Bukszpan, Daniel. *The Encyclopedia of Heavy Metal*. New York, NY: Sterling Publishing, 2003.

Christe, Ian. *Sound of the Beast: The Complete Headbanging History of Heavy Metal*. New York, NY: HarperCollins, 2004.

Koopmans, Andy. *The Osbournes* (People in the News). New York, NY: Gale Group, 2003.

Osbourne, Sharon, with Penelope Dening. *Extreme: My Autobiography*. New York, NY: Grand Central Publishing, 2006.

Saucerman, Linda. *Ozzy Osbourne and Kelly Osbourne* (Famous Families). New York, NY: Rosen Publishing Group, 2004.

Weinstein, Deena. *Heavy Metal: The Music and Its Culture*. New York, NY: Da Capo Press, 2000.

BIBLIOGRAPHY

Bukszpan, Daniel. *The Encyclopedia of Heavy Metal*. New York, NY: Sterling Publishing, 2003.

IMDB.com. "Biography for Sharon Osbourne." Retrieved November 25, 2007 (http://www.imdb.com/name/nm0651769/bio).

M&C News. "Ozzfest 2007 Makes History—Livenation.com Distributes 428,000 Tickets." Retrieved November 25, 2007 (http://musicmonsterandcritics.com/new/article_1318237.pnp).

MTV.com. "Meet the Family: Sharon." Retrieved November 25, 2007 (http://www.mtv.com/onair/osbournes/hub_sharon2.jhtml).

SMN.com. "Ozzfest—Date Lineup History from 1996." Retrieved November 23, 2007 (http://www.smnnews.com/ozzfest-date-lineup-history-from-1996).

INDEX

B
Battle for Ozzfest, 22
Black Label Society, 15, 21
Black Sabbath, 5, 10, 12–13, 30, 32

D
Danzig, 8, 37
Davis, Jonathan, 29

F
Family Values Tour, 42
Fear Factory, 5, 8, 10
first-aid tent personnel, 29

H
Halford, Rob, 9
heavy metal, types of, 9–10

I
Iron Maiden, 5, 10, 21, 32

J
Judas Priest, 5, 9, 10, 32

K
Kittie, 5, 6, 10, 21, 33
Korn, 10, 21, 29, 42

L
Lander, Mercedes, 33–35
Lander, Morgan, 5, 33–35

M
merchandise vendors, 29
Motörhead, 5, 10, 15

O
Osbourne, Ozzy, 5, 6, 7, 8, 10, 11–14, 15, 20, 22, 23–24, 25, 37, 41
Osbourne, Sharon (née Arden), 5, 7, 12, 13, 14–15, 20, 22, 23–24, 25, 37, 41
Osbournes, The, 12, 13, 14
Ozzfest, creation of, 7, 15

P
Pantera, 5, 10, 21, 32, 34
Prong, 8, 37

R
Rockstar Taste of Chaos, 41–42

S
Slayer, 5, 8, 10, 21
Slipknot, 6, 15, 21
sound engineers, 28
St. Hubbins, David, 9

T
Tool, 5, 10, 21
tour caterers, 29
tour promoters, 25–26
tour security, 28

47

tour truck drivers, 26–27

V
Victor, Tommy, 37–38

Z
Z., Brent, 35–36
Zombie, Rob, 10, 21

About the Author

Greg Robison has been actively involved in the music industry for the past fifteen years. He is the cofounder of an independent record label, has served as a band manager and consultant, and has promoted numerous concerts and special music events. In addition to this title, Robison is the author of *Vans Warped Tour*; *Coachella*; and *Christian Rock Festivals*, all published by Rosen. He and his wife, Kelly, live in Texas.

Photo Credits

Cover, p. 1 © Getty Images; back cover © www.istockphoto.com/Milan Klusacek; pp. 4 (left), 21, 36 © Joe Giron/Corbis, pp. 4 (right), 26, 27, 30 © Tim Mosenfelder/Getty Images; p. 8 © Charles Langella/Corbis; p. 11 © Chris Walter/WireImage/Getty Images; p. 13 © MTV/Everett Collection; p. 14 © Stuart Wilson/Getty Images; p. 17 © Jason Moore/Zuma Press; p. 19 © Vaughn Youtz/Zuma Press; p. 24 © Chad Buchanan/Getty Images; p. 28 © Gary Miller/FilmMagic/Getty Images; p. 33 © Lindsay Campbell of BadLuckCity Photography; p. 38 © Marty Temme/WireImage/Getty Images; p. 42 © Paul McConnell/Getty Images.

Designer: Nelson Sá; Editor: Christopher Roberts
Photo Researcher: Marty Levick